B5/01
12/2/0
'6

MY BODY™

My Ears

Kathy Furgang

The Rosen Publishing Group's
PowerKids Press™
New York

For Grandma

Published in 2001 by The Rosen Publishing Group, Inc.
29 East 21st Street, New York, NY 10010

Copyright © 2001 by The Rosen Publishing Group, Inc.

First Edition

Book Design: Kim Sonsky

Illustration Credits: All organ 3-D illustrations © Lifeart/TechPool Studios, Inc.; All other 3-D illustrations by Kim Sonsky.

Furgang, Kathy.
   My ears/by Kathy Furgang.
      p. cm.–(My body)
   Includes index.
   ISBN 0-8239-5572-9 (lib. bdg. : alk. paper)
      1. Ear–Juvenile literature. 2. Hearing–Juvenile literature. I. Title
QP462.2 .F87 2000
612.8'5–dc21   99-058313

Manufactured in the United States of America

Contents

The Ears

What body parts allow you to hear things such as music, dogs barking, or your friends talking? Your ears and your brain work together so that you can hear. Your ears are in charge of sending your brain messages about sound. Your brain gets the messages and lets you know what the sound is and from where it comes. Your brain can tell the difference among thousands of different sounds. A **sense organ** is a body part that helps your brain understand things about the world around you. Your ears, eyes, nose, and mouth are all sense organs.

Like your eyes, nose, and mouth, your ears are sense organs. They send your brain messages about sounds so you can hear a dog barking or your favorite TV show.

How Do We Hear?

Clap your hands. The air around you **vibrated**, or moved, sending a **sound wave** through the air. The sound wave was an up and down movement that traveled through all the parts of your ear. When it reached the farthest part inside your ear, a message was sent to your brain. Your brain sent a message back that said you just heard the sound of clapping hands. This happened in less than a second. Sound travels so fast that it reaches your brain at almost the same moment that it happens.

As these kids play patty cake, sound waves reach the farthest parts inside their ears. The ears then send a message to their brains, letting them know what they heard. All this takes less than a second!

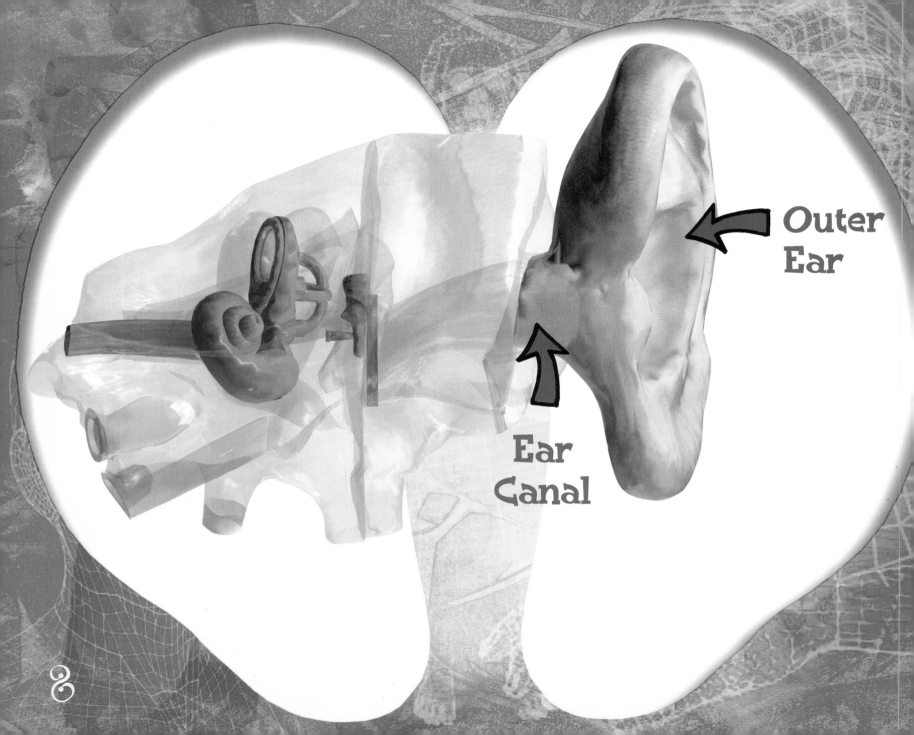

Outer
Ear

Ear
Canal

The Outer Ear

Touch your ear. The part you can feel is called the **auricle**. It is part of your **outer ear**. A hole in the auricle helps bring sound inside your head. Sound reaches many parts of your ear so you can hear. Another part of your outer ear is the **ear canal**. The canal is about one inch long. It reaches inside your **skull**, or head bone. Ear wax is made inside the ear canal. The wax traps dirt so that the inside of your ears stay clean.

he auricle acts like a funnel to bring sound into your ear. The
canal is where ear wax is made. When ear wax builds up,
es, flakes, and comes out of the auricle.

The Middle Ear

Your **middle ear** starts at the end of your ear canal. There is a tight piece of skin there called the **eardrum**. The eardrum moves like a drum when sound hits it. The movement of the eardrum also makes three tiny bones in your middle ear move. These three bones are called ossicles. One of these bones is smaller than a grain of rice! These bones help bring sound farther into your ear. Your middle ear is filled with air because sound waves travel through air. A small tube connects your middle ear to your throat so that your ears always have the right amount of air in them.

The ossicles are the three smallest bones in the human body. They help bring the sounds you hear, like the toot of a horn, farther into your ear.

Eardrum

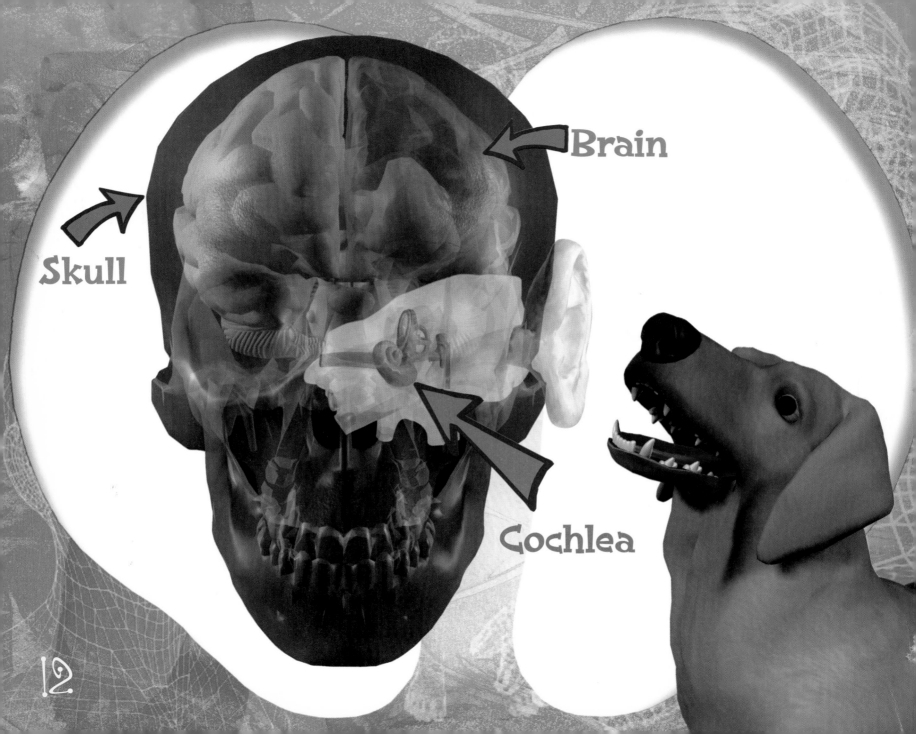

The Inner Ear

When sound finally reaches your **inner ear**, the sound is far inside your skull. The **cochlea** is one of the main parts of your inner ear. This is a tube shaped like a snail shell. There is liquid inside the cochlea, as well as tiny fibers called **nerve cells**. When sound waves travel through liquid in the cochlea, the sound also touches the tiny nerve cells. The nerve cells send messages to your brain. It is your brain that can tell the difference between a doorbell ringing and a dog barking, not your ears.

Inside the cochlea are tiny nerve cells that send messages to the brain. When you hear a dog barking or a car horn, it is your brain that is telling you the difference between these two sounds.

Balance

Your inner ear has another important job besides helping you hear. You are able to keep your balance because of your inner ear. Imagine if you did not know if you were upside down or right side up! There are three tubes, called the **semicircular canals**, that loop above the cochlea. These canals are filled with liquid. When you move your head, the liquid moves, too. When the liquid moves, it touches different nerves that send messages to your brain. Each loop sends the brain messages about a different kind of movement. Up and down movements, side to side movements, and forward and backward movements are all part of your balance.

When you do things that require balance, such as riding a bike or doing a headstand, it is your inner ear that helps you.

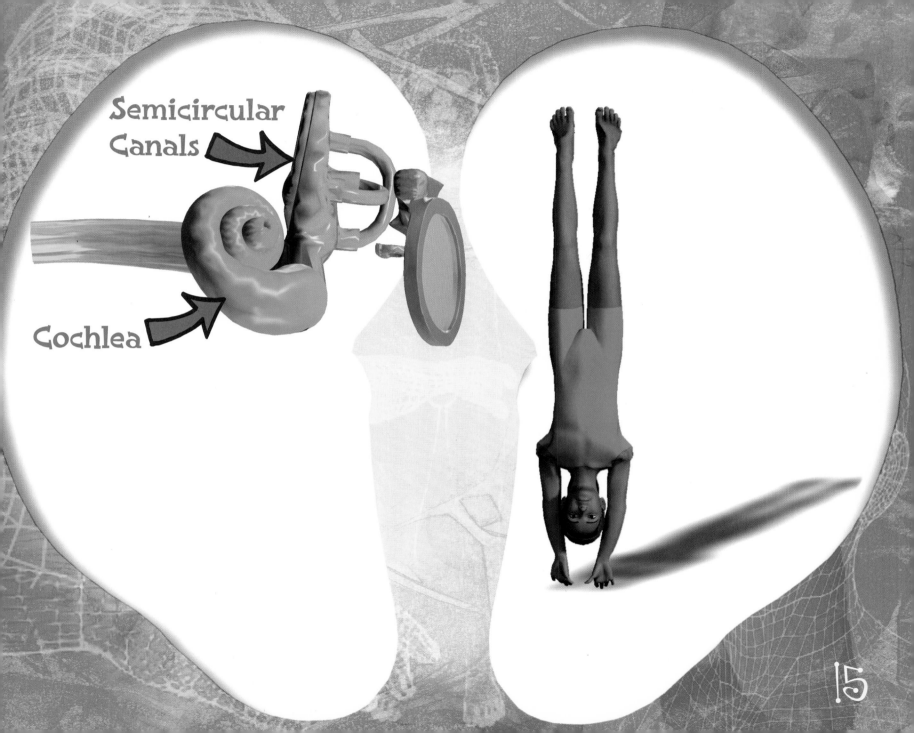

Semicircular
Canals

Cochlea

15

Millions of Sounds

Sounds can be loud or soft. They can also be high or low. We can hear sounds as soft as a whisper. We can hear sounds as loud as a jumbo jet. Some sounds are too loud for our ears to hear safely. If you stand too close to a loud siren, for example, sound waves can break through your thin eardrums. If your eardrums break, they will not be able to do their job. If you feel pain in your ears when you hear a sound, that sound may be harmful to them.

You and a friend can play a fun game. Have one of you cover your eyes and try to figure out what sound the other is making. Then switch places. See how many different sounds you can make out.

Hearing in Other Animals

Many animals can hear much better than we can. The shape of their ears is very important to their hearing. Most dogs have pointed ears that move in different directions to find out from where a sound is coming. Sound waves travel through the air until something blocks or catches them. Rabbits have long ears that catch sound waves. The shape of our ears mainly protects them from dirt and harm. Our ears do not move around like other animals' ears. Some people can wiggle their ears, though. Can you?

Have you noticed that your cat or dog hears noises before you do? One reason animals hear better is because of the shape of their ears. What do you do when you want to hear better?

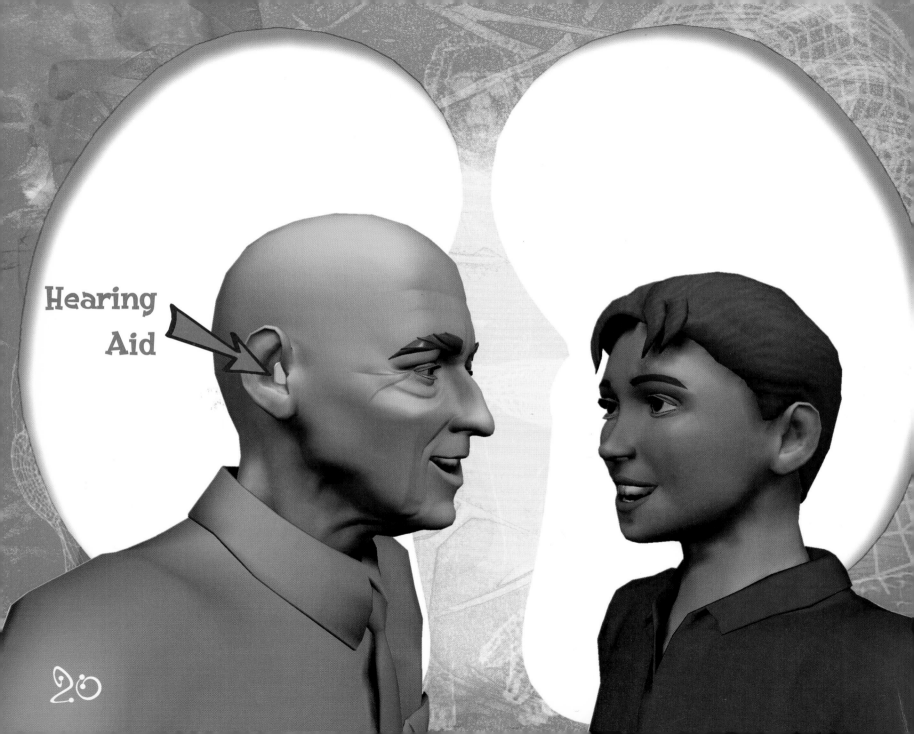

Hearing Aid

Does Everyone Hear the Same Way?

Not everyone's ears are exactly the same. Some people are born with differently shaped outer, middle, or inner ears. This may affect the way they hear. Sometimes people have problems with their ears because of accidents or illnesses. It is natural for some people to hear better than others. One thing that helps people who cannot hear well is an instrument called a hearing aid. Some hearing aids fit in the ear, while others are worn behind the ear. They act like a tiny loudspeaker to help someone hear better.

Illness, an accident, or age can affect a person's hearing. If someone has trouble hearing, he or she might wear a hearing aid.

Living Without Sound

People who are deaf have a lot of trouble hearing sounds. Some deaf people cannot hear any sounds at all. Many deaf people can tell what others are saying by the movement of their lips. This is called **lip reading**. People also use hand signals, called sign language, to **communicate**. Sign language is a language in which hand motions stand for words or ideas. Some televisions have words along the bottom of the screen that show what people on the television are saying. This is called closed captioning. There are many ways in which people who are deaf can get along in a world with sound.

Glossary

auricle (OR-eh-kul) The outer part of the ear that we can see and touch.

cochlea (KOK-lee-ah) A snail-shaped tube with nerve fibers that is found in the inner ear.

communicate (kuh-MYOO-nih-kayt) To share information or feelings.

ear canal (EER kan-AL) The tube that leads into the middle ear.

eardrum (EER-drum) A thin sheet of skin inside the ear that vibrates when sound enters the ear.

inner ear (IN-nur EER) The part of the ear involved with balance and nerve cells.

lip reading (LIP REED-ing) The ability to understand what someone is saying by watching the movement of his or her lips.

middle ear (MID-dul EER) The air-filled part of the ear that contains the eardrum and tiny bones.

nerve cells (NURV SELZ) Tiny fibers that carry information from the brain to places all around the body.

outer ear (OUT-ur EER) Part of the ear that includes the auricle and ear canal.

semicircular canals (SEM-ee-surKUEW-lahr KAN-ahlz) Three tubes in the inner ear that allow us to keep our balance.

sense organ (SENS OR-gan) A body part that helps your brain understand things about the world around you. These include the ears, eyes, nose, and mouth.

skull (SKUL) The bone in an animal's or person's head that protects the brain.

sound wave (SOWND WAYV) The movement of sound through the air.

vibrated (VY-brayt-ed) When something has moved back and forth quickly.

Index

Web Sites

To find out more about hearing, sound, and sign language, check out these Web sites:

http://where.com/scott.net/asl/abc.html
http://www.frontiernet.net/~imaging/play_a_piano.html
http://www.hipmag.org/

24